Small
Guide,
Big
Journey

Small Guide, Big Journey

Beata Bishop

*The pocket companion
to a conscious life*

PETER OWEN PUBLISHERS
LONDON AND CHICAGO

PETER OWEN PUBLISHERS
Conway Hall, 25 Red Lion Square, London WC1R 4RL

Peter Owen books are distributed in the USA and Canada by
Independent Publishers Group/Trafalgar Square
814 North Franklin Street, Chicago, IL 60610, USA

First published by Peter Owen Publishers 2020

PAPERBACK ISBN 978-0-7206-2080-1
EPUB ISBN 978-0-7206-2081-8
MOBIPOCKET ISBN 978-0-7206-2082-5
PDF ISBN 978-0-7206-2083-2

A catalogue record for this book is available from
the British Library

Printed and bound in the UK by
CPI Group (UK) Ltd, Croydon CR0 4YY

Note: When an infant, a child or the concept of the Inner Child is discussed without explicit gender, the pronoun 'it' or 'its' is employed in this book to avoid clumsy 'his or her', 'him or his' or 'their'/'they' constructions.

Contents

Contents

Introduction

'Life is a journey that doesn't begin with birth and doesn't end with the death of the body.' I don't recall where I first read this definition, which accurately describes my own firm belief. To my mind, life has two portals, birth and death, and between the two we learn, stumble, forget, remember; we collect happy moments and bend under the weight of bad times; we love and we hate while travelling along the way. And the main aim of our journey is learning to live consciously.

'The unexamined life is unworthy of a human being,' wrote Plato 2,500 years ago. While in outline our lives have much in common, it is the details that add colour and flavour to each individual existence. This little book is meant to be a modest guide to life's most basic, most widely shared experiences, from early childhood to the final chapter which asks the question 'Is this an end or a beginning?' The choice is ours.

I don't want all this to sound too serious. One of the great gifts of living consciously is the ability to see the difference between our serious and trivial problems and to find the latter frankly ridiculous. Altogether I believe that a sense of humour, the ability to laugh at ourselves, is one of life's greatest bonuses: it dissolves tension, gets things into proportion and, above all, brings physical relief. A few years ago a laughter centre was established in Amsterdam where members dropped in before going to work and spent a few minutes roaring with laughter, for no reason but with total dedication. Then, greatly relaxed and breathing deeply, they went on their way. How about setting up a similar oasis nearer to home?

At any rate, it's time for me to ask the reader to follow the itinerary described in these pages and add its discoveries to his or her precious individual journey.

I
Meet the Inner Child

However old we are, in every single one of us resides an Inner Child that plays an important role within the psyche. Generally we are unaware of its presence, so that it can function totally uncontrolled, producing many unexpected situations. It symbolizes and represents the good and bad qualities of a real child. On the positive side, it is spontaneous, open, trusting and playful, also hugely imaginative, believing in boundless possibilities. Full of love and natural charm, it lives in a magical world of its own making.

On the negative side, it is moody and tends to exaggerate. Ruled by strong urges, it considers itself supremely important and gets very cross if others don't agree. It is also selfish, undisciplined and possessive, reacting with sharp jealousy to real or imaginary rivals. It is a mixture of little angel and little devil, a deeply human creature hiding in us all.

In most of us the Inner Child carries a wound, acquired when we were very young. Even a so-called happy childhood cannot protect us from inner hurts. However good and loving our parents were, sooner or later we found ourselves in a situation in which one or both of them or some other older, stronger person acted in a way that left us feeling wounded.

At the time our child self didn't know how to handle this, how to react and restore a semblance of balance between us and the adult, so the wound remained unhealed. For the psyche, time doesn't count, nor is it a healer, so that early wounds and hurt feelings can survive lifelong in the unconscious unless we consciously begin to heal them.

To use a metaphor, imagine four or five human beings who are born and raised together and develop well, except one child who suffers a wound; as a result its growth comes to a halt. It hides from the others who grow up and lead successful lives, remaining friends. But every now and then something happens that reminds the hiding wounded child of the original trauma, upon which it rushes forward, pushes the others aside, stages a noisy scene and then vanishes again. The others, embarrassed and ashamed, try their best to repair the damage, whether it was due to a so-called Freudian slip, unjustified aggression or a groundless accusation.

This is how the wounded Inner Child functions: without warning it takes over the controls, demands the impossible – and we have to clear up the resulting mess. In other words, it reacts to an adult situation in the manner of a small child. This normally happens in important relationships and may cause serious harm.

As a rule, the Inner Child suffers a narcissistic wound. To understand this, let us consider its origin, the myth of Narcissus, the son of a river god and a nymph, blessed with extraordinary beauty. The blind seer Tiresias told his mother that Narcissus would enjoy a long life on earth only if he never got to know himself.

Youths and maidens all fell in love with Narcissus, but he cruelly rejected them all. The nymph Echo, who could only repeat the words of others, became consumed by sorrow until just her voice survived: that is how she became a disembodied echo. One of the worshippers of Narcissus killed himself out of despair and asked the gods to revenge his death. The goddess Artemis undertook the task and sentenced Narcissus to fall in love with someone who could never belong to him.

One day Narcissus lay down by a brook, the water of

which was as clear as a mirror, and fell in love with his own reflection. After a while he realized that his desire was for himself, but he stayed by the brook, neither eating nor drinking and feeling bitterly unhappy, until finally he stabbed himself to death. His blood fell on the ground and gave rise to a white narcissus. (Herbalists make an ointment from the plant to treat frostbite, as if to cure the emotional frigidity of the original Narcissus.)

That is what the myth tells us. In psychology two kinds of narcissism are defined. One is healthy: this applies to the small child who needs to be acknowledged, taken seriously, mirrored and loved for itself, not for its small achievements. Let us remember what it was like to be small, weak and with no autonomy in a world of giants. Around us everyone except us knew the rules, but we were told off if we made a single mistake. Under the circumstances it was vitally important that our mother or mother figure should mirror us with love and appreciation through her voice and touch, praising our achievements, however small they were, and thus build up our self-confidence.

If this process succeeds, all is well. The Inner Child doesn't suffer the narcissistic wound. It may suffer other hurts, but as its basic self-confidence is sound it knows how to handle difficulties. However, this early process may fail if the mother herself had not received the positive mirroring and praise she needed and therefore carries a narcissistic wound. She cannot expect from her partner what she did not receive from her parents: the past cannot be altered. But with the birth of her own child she feels that at last there is someone who belongs to her, depends on her and will not, cannot, abandon her and who – she believes – will give her everything that had been denied her in the past.

The process is unconscious, but that only makes it more powerful. And, equally unconsciously, the small child adapts to the needs and expectations of the adored mother in order to gain her love. This means denying its real original essence and substituting for it a False Self that will persist into adulthood. For this there is a steep price to pay – a sense of emptiness that no worldly success can heal, a lack of purpose and the homelessness of the psyche. This is the narcissistic wound that one generation passes on to the next, unwittingly and unintentionally.

We cannot change the past, but we can redeem it by contemplating it from a different viewpoint. According to the American adage, 'You can have a happy childhood at any age', and with a bit of luck this can be true. As a first step we need to confront the reality of our child-hood experiences: what was life really like all those years ago? Perhaps we shall need to give up the fantasy of the happy, idyllic childhood we have adopted until now to cover up the less delightful reality. Perhaps we will remember our pain and sorrow of long ago that we have managed to put out of our head until now.

And then there are those who cannot recall anything from their childhood – their earliest memory perhaps goes back only to the age of ten. However, as we never truly forget anything, merely bury it deep in our uncon-scious, we need to ask just what was so intolerable in their childhood that forced them to 'forget' it. This must be handled with great care. Sometimes a simple question unlocks the door, and a tsunami of memories follows.

Giving up the fantasy and confronting the no-longer-forgotten material may be painful, yet the reality must be faced, partly in our own interest, partly for the sake of our loved ones. All the negative stuff we are unaware of will be projected on to others and may lead to hypocrisy: consider the comment of Jesus about the man who looks at the speck in his brother's eye but doesn't notice the log in his own. Here, however, we are not dealing with hypocrisy but with unconscious projection.

One kind of projection comes into being if a small child who has no siblings or whose parents do not fulfil its emotional needs projects the missing feelings on to an imaginary playmate or a doll or a toy. That's why the child's favourite puppet or teddy bear should never be thrown out, however worn or dirty it is: it may mean more to the child than the adults suspect. A nice clean substitute may be offered – and rejected because it lacks the old magic.

Another projection occurs when the small child doesn't yet have a strong ego and unwittingly takes on the repressed problem of one of its parents. The so-called neurotic problems of a child almost without exception originate in the unconscious processes of its parents. If the parents solve their own problems, the child's difficulties normally vanish. For instance, when one particularly violent, unsociable small boy was taken along to a child psychologist it swiftly became clear that his parents were constantly quarrelling and that his mother had smashed up three ironing-boards in the heat of arguments.

Whatever happens to the child leaves a trace and begins

to shape the Inner Child of the future who normally gets stuck at the age when it suffered a wounding event. The small child reacts instinctively to the parents' unexpressed inner processes; its unconscious is linked to theirs. That's why the adults should always be honest and open with the child and not pretend to be perfect.

The adult's demand of obedience creates another tricky situation. Two wills clash: the one based on endurance is going to win. If the child gives in only after a lengthy and stormy altercation which it has secretly enjoyed, it may use this irrational, over-emotional and stormy method against its partner in adulthood. Yet what has worked reasonably well for a four- or five-year-old may cause a major crisis thirty years later.

How do we see our Inner Child if we set aside today's adult awareness? What was it most afraid of then and there? What worried it most? Did it get any help, perhaps from an imaginary playmate or mentor like Cinderella's fairy godmother? Perhaps we fantasized about an ideal parent; perhaps some toy, doll or magical pebble represented a supernatural power that protected us.

This is where the so-called transitional object comes into its own. It can be anything: a piece of clothing, an outgrown cap or sock or a small piece of an old blanket that the child holds on to day and night. Already getting a foretaste of autonomy, the individual is moving away very slightly from the mother but is still unable to let go of the link that represents safety. Hence the child's frantic clinging to the transitional object, until one day he or she throws it away or loses it.

In all this, imagination has a decisive role to play – imagining what isn't there, concealing what causes pain, do as if . . . This is the secret and the use of magical thinking. Is it possible that under the influence of a powerful emotional storm, stress or pressure we still find refuge in these methods? The only difference being that today smoking, drinking, using illegal drugs or over-eating are substitutes for the outgrown sock.

Imagination offers a practical way to heal the wounded Inner Child. All it needs is a batch of our childhood photographs taken before our sixth birthday. We pick the one that we react to most vividly and which depicts us on our own. The others can be set aside.

Now let us concentrate on the picture of our choice. Let us remember where it was taken, what the occasion was, what memories it evokes and record whatever comes to mind. This photograph will guide us to find our wounded Inner Child. We keep it by our bedside, greet the Child on wakening and wish it good night before falling asleep. During the day, too, when we have a few free moments, we speak to the Child or listen to what it may have to tell us. Let us do this daily until we have established a close friendship with this entity who belongs to our existence.

Most importantly, in the midst of stress, strong feelings or a major upset, we imagine for a moment that our Inner Child is standing next to us. We hold its hand and say to it, 'I understand. I know what you feel, but let me deal with this situation – me, the adult, not you. Afterwards we'll talk about it.'

This simple spell is the key to healing the wounded Inner Child: it provides the understanding, caring and love it has been longing for all its life. Once it has been healed, it will start offering its gifts: spontaneity, huge vitality, joy, playfulness, the simple enjoyment of small things. Perhaps this is the moment to choose some creative hobby that will express our new gifts.

And don't let us forget that in today's conflict-ridden and rudderless world a huge number of apparently well-functioning adults are sheltering and living with a hurt Inner Child. Let us remember that in difficult moments, when the other person is taken over by a furious, embittered or distraught Inner Child, it needs us, as understanding adults, to defuse the situation calmly and in a spirit of friendship.

2

The Mother

*'Maternal love is one of life's most moving and most unfor-
gettable memories; it is the mysterious root of all growth
and change. This love means a homecoming and a refuge,
and the long silence in which everything has its beginning
and its end.' – Carl Gustav Jung*

Already, on biological grounds, we have a deep, basic and
lifelong connection to our mother, because of the huge
difference between the birth of humans and non-
humans. As soon as a foal, a calf or a zebra is born, it
stands up at once, gets fed by its mother and fairly soon
starts an independent existence alongside its parent. By
contrast, the human embryo develops over nine months,
undergoes a painful birth and remains totally dependent
on its mother for a long time. Hence, right from the start
mother and child have a unique essential connection that

can be good, bad, inadequate or variable. What is certain is that its quality will have a decisive effect on the child's development.

'Mmmmm' – this sound, resembling the baby's reaction to being fed, is connected with the word 'mother' in many languages: mama, mamma, Mutter, mère, Demeter (goddess) and many more. The mythical and symbolic Great Mother guards the two portals of life. She is an archetype living in our deep unconscious, representing a shared human experience over countless millennia. We call her, we recognize her, and sometimes we mix her up with our real human mother whom we credit with superhuman powers to our mutual detriment. The mother doesn't create life, she just passes it on, but our story did have a beginning at some stage, as described in the ancient creation myths.

These tell us that in the beginning there was just night and darkness. The Planet Earth was a bleak desert, nothing but squelchy mud and fermentation, yet it gave birth to all living things once oxygen came into being, enabling life proper to begin. In an unimaginable cosmic drama the universe was born, bringing forth the many children of the dark ancestral Mother – the Sun, the Moon, the stars and the planets; then life appeared on

Earth, producing plants, animals and humans, until much later consciousness arose from the human unconscious, and the great nothingness gave birth to the gods.

What we know about the cult of the Great Mother comes from archaeological finds, some of them 40,000 years old. In the huge area stretching from Siberia to the Pyrenees identical statues have been discovered, carved from animal bones or stone, representing the heavily pregnant goddess with her small head and disproportionately large, pendulous breasts. The best examples survive in Malta, Sicily and the Cyclades, all of them islands with ancient caves long regarded as sanctuaries.

The Father God, Lord of the Sun and of consciousness, appeared much later. According to the Sumerian myth, the creator of the world was the Great Mother Tiamat who was defeated and cut to pieces by her great-grandson Marduk. However, Tiamat's body became the foundation of the sky and of the underworld; thus she continued to contain the universe. The ancient Great Mother seems invincible.

Similar myths came into being later in other parts of the world. In essence, they all claim that the primeval feminine is awakened or conquered by the primeval masculine in order to create the world. The son of the

24

goddess is also her husband; he is sacrificed every year but comes back to life.

The Mother Goddess has her positive and negative sides. When positive, she gives birth, protects and nourishes. Her symbols are the pot, the jug or the large dish that contains food or a dead body. She carries her child on her back, she feeds and cherishes it, and her love is limitless. When negative, she is witch, vampire, dragon, gaping tomb, death, abyss and void. The goddesses of war and of the hunt belong here, among them the Indian goddess Kali who dances on a corpse wearing a necklace made from human skulls. Yet around her the Earth is producing new green shoots.

In Egypt and ancient Greece the mystery of the Mother Goddess evoked fear and respect. The Greek Demeter as the good mother guarded the portal of birth in the east; the goddess Hecate guarded the western portal of death. Even the negative myths expressed their dark message in poetic style.

In Christianity Eve is the source of every possible trouble, while the Blessed Virgin Mary represents every possible virtue. Jung called the Virgin Mother an impossible ideal and model for Catholic women to follow. As if to counterbalance this, today over 450 Black Madonnas exist all over the world. Modern scholars identify these with pre-Christian goddesses such as Isis or Artemis. Official Church sources claim that these Madonnas were blackened by centuries of candle smoke – but, if this is so, why are their clothes and cloaks blazing with rich colour? Black Madonnas have always attracted countless pilgrims. When the Church authorities had some of them painted white the pilgrims no longer came.

We need to appreciate the specific atmosphere of a myth: it hints at the presence of an archetype, in countless disguises but with the same single meaning. In different phases of life the Great Mother may be symbolized by a wide range of women: mother, grandmother, stepmother, nurse, nanny and teacher may all assume her role.

Her positive qualities include caring, wisdom, authority, goodwill and everything else that promotes growth and creativity. Her negative side contains all that is dark, hidden, secret, toxic, seductive and confining.

'In the individual psyche the mother is hugely significant,' wrote Jung, yet he ascribed limited importance to the real-life mother. Her impact on the child came not just from her personally but from the archetype projected on to her, and this was the source of her mythical aura, great authority and power.

Every baby experiences the primeval duality of the positive and negative, kind and monstrous mother. In its pre-conscious state the newborn infant does not differentiate between itself and the mother or, rather, the nursing breast, provided that it is well cared for and receives milk immediately when hungry.

In the beginning the newborn baby enjoys a kind of omnipotence: all its wishes had been fulfilled in the womb's Paradise. However, it quickly realizes that it is no longer in Paradise, nor is it identical with the mother or the breast, and its wishes sometimes remain unfulfilled. It acquires the concept of the good and bad mother, good and bad breast, and later realizes that the two belong together. The baby must get used to being frustrated, to not being omnipotent and to the good mother sometimes being cruel. If the mother leaves the room, the baby wonders whether she'll return, because if she doesn't the baby will perish. Hence the earth-shattering rages of very small infants.

According to the famous English paediatrician and psychoanalyst Donald Winnicott (1896–1971), mother and infant should be seen as one unit, not discussed separately. The adult's character, development and ability to relate depend on the quality of this early relationship, which must therefore be taken seriously and given full attention.

It was Winnicott who defined the three categories of maternal attitudes as the too-good mother, the bad mother and the ideal good-enough mother. The baby's first connection with the mother is through the body: through her touch and smell and her two arms holding the baby. The answer to Winnicott's question 'How is she holding it?' determines to which category the mother belongs.

The hold of the good-enough mother is secure, steady, neither too tight nor too loose. During the child's first five years, within wise limits she dedicates herself to its care. Between the ages of five and twelve she encourages the child to start exploring the outside world and develop its own ego. The father's role grows more important. The child knows that come what may it will be loved. It needs continuity, a regular lifestyle, gentle guidance and the correct handling of anger.

With puberty the child's ego continues to develop well, but it is still firmly rooted in the home. The good-enough mother provides support, while also letting go of her child. The child becomes aware of the feminine side of life. The boy isn't afraid of it; the girl accepts it with ease. At the start of adult life this kind of young person steps out gladly into the outside world with openness and sociability. The child who in the first five years of life was held and handled firmly yet gently by its mother will be able to cope with all difficulties in later life.

The too-good mother spoils the child and does not prepare it for the outside world, which will not provide the same level of love and caring. The too-tight holding expresses the mother's unfulfilled physical and emotional needs. She wants her child to remain young and small; she holds back its development and doesn't let it go. The atmosphere she creates is choking and absorbing. As an adult this child never achieves its aims: in the last moment it stops abruptly, because something draws it back to its mother, as if it were held back by a rubber band or a silken cobweb. The umbilical cord is invisibly present.

The daughter may find it difficult to separate her own femininity from that of the mother. Irrespective of age, she may permanently remain a young girl whose sexuality stays dormant.

The son may come to believe the mother's claim that all men are brutal, insensitive beings, hence his own masculinity may not develop fully.

Sons and daughters may have homosexual tendencies; it may be that they are looking for the mother and are able to establish relationships only with members of their own gender.

The hold of the bad mother is too loose or non-existent, which awakens in the baby the atavistic fear of falling. The mother is emotionally immature, with an unformed personality; her loosely held infant is terrified of being dropped and abandoned. Growing up, it is timid and insecure with no sense of being firmly rooted in life or linked to its own body and instincts. Its self-image is indistinct and ill-defined.

If the bad mother's child is of a passive disposition, it tends to lead a fantasy life, analysing the past or making guesses about the future, while neglecting the present. It is timid, self-punishing, needing an inordinate amount of encouragement and support. Over-loving potential part-ners ruins its relationships, so does its hyper-sensitivity to criticism, with a tendency to sulk and act the silent martyr. Its weakness has a power of its own which makes stronger people feel brutal by comparison. It attempts to turn all love affairs into a parent–child relationship.

The active type was also held too loosely, but this one rebels and serves a cause or an ideal. Here there's no link between head and heart, no respect for others' personal space, only fear of feelings and of physical relationships.

Dominant personalities both attract and frighten this type who only appears to be strong, needing an inordinate amount of love to make it acknowledge its weakness and accept feelings. The sense of insecurity of the first phase of its life may overshadow the subsequent years and decades.

The above descriptions are deliberately exaggerated; their aim is to emphasize our potential mistakes so that we may avoid or, if need be, remedy them. Let us not concentrate too much on the past. Our task is to understand what can cause an early wound, how an early mother–child connection can go wrong. But the problem of the subsequent relationship is just as important, the process by which the grown-up child separates from the mother and establishes a new, more independent connection with her, ideally that of the loving but autonomous link between two adults. The task of the daughter is to discover and nurture her feminine self and accept that it may drastically differ from the maternal model. Similarly, the task of the son is to become aware of his concept of the feminine and make sure that the maternal 'shadow' dwelling in his unconscious does not invade his love relationships.

Needless to say, in all these matters the mother's attitude

is hugely important. If she is lonely and has an unsatisfactory partner or none, she may seek compensation through her children and make their bond too tight. This may bring untold trouble and unhappiness to all concerned. But the wise and truly loving mother is able to release her children, safe in the certainty that their heartfelt link will always last undiminished through space and time.

3
The Father

'According to Freud, all so-called divine figures originate in the father-image. This would be hard to deny; however, we have something else to say about the father-image itself. The parental image has an extraordinary effect; it influences the child's psyche to such an extent that the question arises: can this magical power be ascribed to an ordinary human being?' – Carl Gustav Jung

Today the role of the father is largely determined by location. In traditional patriarchal societies the father is almost omnipotent. Even if he migrates to a modern country in the developed world, he remains the head of the family who tolerates no contradiction. With or without the help of his sons he may even kill his daughter if she wishes to marry a man of whom he doesn't approve. Such cases are briefly and disapprovingly reported by the

Western press, but it's only a matter of time before another similar tragedy occurs.

At the opposite end of the polarity, in developed countries the father plays an active role in the life of the family. He takes care of the children, including a newborn baby; except for nursing, he is able to act as a mother substitute. The contrast between the two attitudes could hardly be sharper: it results from the way the social roles of men and women have changed over the past few decades. Women now enjoy greater autonomy, increased financial independence and more successful careers. Even if they are paid less than men for the same kind of work, this inequality is now a matter of public debate. Also, if both partners, married or otherwise, take equal shares of supporting and caring for their family, they are granted equal rights.

This of course also has its shadow side: domestic violence against women has become more frequent in families where the dethroned men express their rage and confusion with sheer brutality. After countless millennia of male dominance, it is difficult for men to assume a new role and transform the essence of fatherhood. Divorce has become endemic. There are huge numbers of single parents, mainly mothers, who bring up their children alone, and, however well a single mother performs her job, she cannot make up for the missing father. This results in a sense of deficiency: there is no masculine example, no clear direction to influence the individual as well as the collective. Although the father's role has diminished, the patriarchy as a system persists. Even so, the picture isn't entirely negative; the public discussion of the topic is a sign of impending change.

To get a complete view of the subject, let us start at the very beginning, with the basic myth that is a poetical attempt to understand the world. Except for Judaism and Christianity, all the ancient creation myths begin with the existence and creation of the Ur-Mother. She is a dark goddess – night and darkness, the underworld and the Earth itself belong to her. According to the myth, 'in the beginning' there was only the darkness, the bleak, watery, muddy soil. Today science confirms the mythical image: the Evolution House in the world-famous botanical gardens at Kew in London presents the earliest origin as an expanse of bubbling, fermenting mud.

In a psychological sense this refers to the underworld of the unconscious, but it is from there that consciousness arises and also the Sun, the Moon and the stars. The cult of the Ur-Mother ruled the matriarchy and left behind a rich collection of artefacts – carvings, statues and sanctu-aries dating back some 12,000 years.

Matriarchy was based on peaceful existence and the cult of the goddess. It also laid the foundation of agricul-ture. Men played an inferior role. Located in the eastern Mediterranean, in a perfect climate and under ideal circumstances, this community enjoyed a long flowering. According to a cynical modern historian, if it had survived we would still be waiting for someone to invent the wheel.

The masculine conquerors – fighters, destroyers, followers of the Storm God – invaded from the north. Myths also began to present a male god and a divine father-figure who either married or conquered the Ur-Mother. Either way this move took forward the great work of creation that was to produce a new version of the world.

From then onwards the masculine deity gradually comes into the foreground. By the time we reach Greek prehistory, he rules the scene, although sometimes he comes to grief. The myth recounts that Uranus, the cold, contemptuous sky god, embraces Gaia, the earth goddess, every night, but he hates the children born from their marriage and hides them deep underground. Gaia cannot bear this. She makes a sharp sickle, gives it to her youngest son Cronus and orders him to castrate his father. Cronus obeys, throws his father's genitals into the sea, upon which Aphrodite, the goddess of beauty, love and harmony, magically rises from the waves.

Thus the castrated tyrannical father disappears and his son Cronus takes over his rule, He marries Rhea, and then, following his father's example, he swallows his children because he fears that one of them may turn against him. The rest of the myth doesn't belong to our subject. The question arises whether Freud didn't misinterpret the Oedipus complex, as our story shows that it isn't only the father who fears his son who might take over his role but the son may also fear his father who might castrate him.

With some adjustments all this can apply to contemporary family situations. The Cronus-type father forbids, limits, insists on the rules, clings to the values of the past and tolerates no contradiction. The son in his own role as a father unconsciously adopts the habits, principles and tone of voice of the dreaded or sometimes even hated father, until one day he realizes what's going on and deliberately severs the inter-generational link.

The myth of Danaë presents three kinds of fatherhood. Acrisius, the king of Argos, has an only daughter,

Danaë. A seer tells him that his grandson will kill him, so he locks up his daughter in a subterranean cell lined with bronze, where, he thinks, no one would find her. However, the all-seeing omnipotent Father God Zeus becomes enamoured of the beautiful girl and impregnates her in the form of golden rain. A boy is born and is named Perseus (Destroyer).

The selfish and cruel Acrisius puts Danaë and her baby in a wooden chest and throws it into the sea. A fisherman catches the chest and takes it to Polidectes, king of the island of Serifos, who gives them shelter. Danaë refuses to marry Polidectes. When Perseus reaches adulthood, Polidectes wants to get rid of him and sends him off to get the head of Medusa, the only mortal of the three monstrous Gorgons.

Since Medusa's eyes turn anyone who dares to meet her gaze to stone, the gods decide to protect Perseus. He receives a dazzling shield from Athena, winged sandals, a sickle-shaped sword and a magical bag from Hermes and the helmet of invisibility from Hades. Aided by this perfect equipment he kills and beheads Medusa. Flying back towards Argos he catches sight of Andromeda and kills the sea monster who keeps her captive.

Brandishing the head of Medusa, he turns all his

enemies to stone and with Danaë and Andromeda returns to Argos where an athletic competition is in full swing. Perseus joins in and throws a discus, which accidentally kills Acrisius. Thus the prophecy is fulfilled. Even a king cannot escape his fate.

Gorgophone, the daughter of Perseus and Andromeda, is the first woman to defy the rules of the patriarchy: when her husband dies she refuses to burn to death on his funeral pyre.

This myth presents the three forms of fatherhood. Acrisius is the cruel, tyrannical father, Zeus is the fructifying, protective kind, while Perseus represents the heroic new model of fatherhood. This is the most coherent myth of the subject. With the exception of Zeus, fatherhood plays no role in the love stories of the Greek gods. They represent the fertilizing masculine principle, and their innumerable affairs produce innumerable offspring, but bringing them up remains the mothers' job.

Among archetypes, Zeus comes nearest to the father ideal: he is powerful and lays down the law, he protects but also punishes and is omniscient. His anger is terrifying; only his wife is able to control him to a certain extent. Strict but just towards his children, his role is to introduce the Logos, the physical, intellectual and spiritual consciousness into the family where at first the mother represented the Eros function, comprising instinct, emotion and intuition, and passed it on to her children.

The father represents the outside world, away from the home. His values include activity, achievement, initiative, order, self-control, discipline, work and security. According to the American psychologist Abraham Maslow, on the pyramid of human needs the two uppermost layers, those of self-esteem and self-actualization, belong to the masculine area.

The English child psychologist John Bowlby maintained that in the first year of life the newborn baby establishes a close emotional link with its mother which gives the child a sense of inner security. All other relationships are of secondary importance. This is what the father has to break up later in order to lead the child, aged three to five years, into the greater world. This doesn't always take place or succeed, with damaging consequences.

The positive father strengthens the child's self-confidence and teaches it how to initiate new things, solve problems and make up its mind. He serves as a good example, sets up the desirable standards and helps the child to discover its own role in life.

The negative father is emotionally immature and

authoritarian. His main function is to forbid, chide and criticize. He damages the child's free spirit and creativity. He is a bully, doesn't listen to others and insists on being right. All this is highly damaging to his children.

The boy child doesn't discover his true self. There is a constant conflict between his real nature and the way he is forced to behave. His sexuality gets distorted, with fantasy being more satisfying than reality. He may be attracted by pornography.

The healthy sexuality and libido of the girl child becomes suppressed. It is as if the tyrannical father regarded her as his own. Past puberty he calls her immoral if she even looks at a boy or wears a short skirt. By contrast, the girl may go through several affairs without any emotional involvement, as if wanting to spite her father. Eventually she marries a man who in many ways resembles her father. In essence she projects him on to every man she meets.

The absent father has either abandoned his family or is separated from the home by his work. Alternatively he may be so weak or withdrawn that his presence is negligible. The mother is often angry and aggressive, assuming the role of a negative father, or else she plays the part of a martyr and makes her children feel guilty. The father principle becomes worthless, it lacks all authority, but in the case of a weak father there is a lot of denied anger and violence to poison the atmosphere.

As a result, the son becomes timid and anxious; he often feels unable to act, and his self-awareness fails to develop. The daughter is either too feminine, out of touch with her own masculine energy and totally under her mother's influence or, in the course of time, she becomes an angry man-hater.

The dead father remains a mystery up to a point. His child didn't know him and compensates for this by idealizing and turning him into an ideal hero, based on marvellous figures from fiction and fantasy. This father has no negative side and exists solely as an almost inimitable model.

If all goes well, his son successfully emulates that imaginary example. Otherwise he will fail, because the standard is too high, leaving him permanently dissatisfied with himself. His daughter falls in love with her concept of the unknown dead father. In adult life she ruins her relationships by chasing an impossible ideal and finding no man to be good enough for her.

These negative types are, once again, deliberately exaggerated. In reality there is a majority of positive, good-enough fathers who educate and guide their children without any hint of dictatorship and who don't ever try to seem perfect. Let us remember that human nature is best described by the principle of 'and also' not of 'either/or', and so in all of us, not just in all fathers, the light and the shadow and all possible emotional polarities belong together inseparably. That's why love, acceptance and a sense of humour are the indispensable tools to make life more than just bearable.

4
A New Look at Relationships

The deception started with the fairy-tales. As children we believed every word of them: the heroine, whether princess or shepherdess, was always beautiful, good and kind; the hero, who likewise came from a variety of backgrounds, was always a paragon of masculine virtues; and these two rare specimens were linked by indestructible love from the moment they met. Yes, they lived happily ever after, because for both of them the other one was the Magical Other, the only possible partner till the end of time.

This is how the concept of the Magical Other entered our credulous minds and hearts, and even later, in our teens, when we had survived several disappointments, we still believed and expected that one day this person will appear (girls awaited this with great zeal, boys had other preoccupations). And from then onwards everything will be wonderful for ever after.

Well, time passed, and eventually it became clear that

the Magical Other didn't exist. This truth is hard to accept, even for people in the second half of life who are solidly married or otherwise linked to a partner and who have long ago abandoned the dreams of their youth. And yet, even so, perhaps only half-consciously, something remains alive deep in their hearts . . . the memory of a memory, a nostalgic sigh or perhaps a melancholy regret for life not fulfilling their expectations.

But if the Magical Other doesn't exist, what is there instead? Well, perhaps a new kind of human relationship; primarily that of a couple, but with some adjustments this can also be applied to other important links, such as the one between parent and child.

With every important close relationship we need to ask whether the two people concerned turn towards each other or, turned inwards, both are expecting the other to provide their narcissistic happiness. That means the girl in love who expects her man to admire, praise and adore her all the time, and the enamoured man who wants his beloved to see him as the greatest, strongest and most brilliant man in the whole world. But the lonely, aimless parent, usually a mother, who wants to live, enjoy and direct her adult daughter's life also belongs here. In fact, the grown-up child would be willing to invite her lonely, depressed mother into her existence and show her that the world is full of interesting and beautiful things – but the mother will only play on her own terms, otherwise she will sulk and withdraw into her shell. In all fairness, often both parties are at fault in this kind of situation.

In a real and realistic relationship the two partners look at and see each other, they listen to and hear each other, instead of delivering their separate monologues. They don't indulge in the equivalent of decorating a Christmas tree, namely the projection of embellishing but also distorting illusions on to each other. At the same time their exaggerated romantic hopes also fade away. Both partners learn to see the other clearly, complete with their good and bad qualities, and then each one can decide whether to establish a relationship with the other.

If a conflict arises, it is just as important for each partner to take responsibility for their contribution to the problem. This can be quite awkward. Relationships that just bumble along tend to be ruled by subjectivity. Things are going badly? Of course, the other one is at fault. I am the plaintiff, the innocent, ill-treated victim . . .

In my work as a psychotherapist I have listened to countless monologues of this kind over the years, and when the flood of complaints ceased I asked just one question: 'And what was your role in all this?' That never went down well. '*My* role?' came the indignant reply. Well, yes. After all, it takes two to tango.

But what if one's partner refuses to cooperate? Ah, that's his or her responsibility, but the one who has reached a degree of clarity must maintain it at all costs. It's a well-established fact that if one half of a closely linked couple begins to change, in time the other half will also change to a certain extent. For better or worse? That depends. If it's for worse, then the other may break off the relationship – or not. Sometimes a compromise must be made, but there's no need for either partner to become a victim. Anyway, nobody becomes a victim without agreeing to assume that role.

The new way also implies that we accept the Other's otherness. We don't expect him or her to see the world and react to events the way we do. This goes without saying, or at least it should. But that's not what we normally do. In the famous musical *My Fair Lady* the protagonist Professor Higgins plaintively sings, 'Why can't a woman be more like a man?'

Well, she can't. But if she could Professor Higgins would get deeply confused. Joking apart, the task of the Chinese symbols Yin and Yang is to create one whole while remaining two separate units. Both contain a small portion of the other, but each one's identity stays the same. After all, the task of individuation, of inner development has to be achieved personally by each one of us.

Antoine de St Exupéry, the author of *The Little Prince*, wrote, 'Love means two people together looking outward in the same direction.' They look outwards, together. They don't turn the relationship into a cage. Love and togetherness has to be nurtured and cared for to make sure it doesn't sink into boredom and over-familiarity. 'They lived happily ever after' is easily misunderstood to mean that for the next thirty or sixty years everything remains unchanged, like the petal or tiny insect preserved in a piece of amber.

In the past twenty or thirty years it was largely women who have been working on their inner development: 80 or sometimes 95 per cent of workshop and seminar participants in this area have been women. Not that they have more time to spare. The true reason is that while men are governed by their brain's rational, logical left hemisphere, for women the right hemisphere adds the full range of emotions, intuition and instinct to the workings of the left, and the work of inner development can't be based purely on rationality and logic. This scares many men away. A good example of this is a couple who decided to experiment with meditation. The wife began to meditate daily and soon noticed an improvement in her daily life: she was calmer and more serene than before, difficulties didn't make her explode and she could fully enjoy happy moments. Her husband noticed and appreciated the changes, but it didn't occur to him to take up meditation himself. Instead he bought a book on the subject, read it – and that was the end of his involvement.

What's the solution? Certainly no missionary attempt at conversion. This is where the need to respect the Other's otherness comes into its own, even if we don't approve of the outcome. Work on one's development should be done quietly, independently, without trying to drag anybody else into the process. According to yoga wisdom, 'Do not waken the sleepers; they will wake up in their own time.'

Over the years I have met many 'unmatched' couples, both as clients and as acquaintances. At best, the partners agreed that although they did not travel on the same inner road this was acceptable – there was no need to live, so to speak, in each other's pockets and share everything totally and constantly. Symbiotic relationships are only acceptable and necessary between infants and their mothers, not between adults. At worst, these couples lurched from one conflict to the next (one of them ended up in the divorce court) The over-dependent clinging individual could not bear that the partner was following another road, moreover one that he or she didn't understand.

The question arises as to what individuation has to do with better, more satisfying and intimate relationships. Well, one depends on the other. Through individuation we are striving to achieve wholeness. According to Jung we never achieve it completely, but what matters is the striving and the journey. The more we are able to reconcile the opposites in ourselves, the light and the shadow, the noble energies and their selfish, inferior versions, the more clearly we realize that our fallible self also contains a divine spark, the richer our lives will be. In time we shall discover that part of the psyche which is the miniature version of the opposite sex: according to Jung, the female psyche contains the Animus, which incorporates masculine dynamism, sense of purpose, logical thinking and initiative, while the male psyche accommodates the Anima, the instinct, intuition, tenderness, patience, devotion and love that belong to the feminine principle.

The social and educational system of the developed world ignores these two complementary aspects. Both sexes must be one thing or another: boys must be masculine, girls feminine; full stop. We need to engage in individual work to discover and reclaim our lost components, in order to build our relationships on new foundations. Let us realize that the Magical Other, the subject of our lifelong quest, is present within ourselves: we need only to recognize and to consciously live with it.

This will make us more complete. We shall no longer look for the desired completeness and union where it doesn't and can't exist, namely, in another human being who has his or her life's task and path that differs from ours. That means the ability to relate more easily to each other, without impossible expectations, sharing what can be shared, whether it's daily bread or sky-high passion; but meanwhile remaining ourselves, offering our partner the best in us, spiced with the less brilliant reality. This kind of link grants inner freedom to both partners, while, in the words of St Exupéry, they look together outwards in the same direction.

Last but not least, there remains the vital subject of conflict resolution. Conflict is timeless and everlasting, born from the tension of opposites. Two wills, two interests, two convictions and two egos clash. It began in the Garden of Eden, when God's prohibition clashed with

Eve's curiosity. It continued when Cain killed his brother Abel, and today on the main road where two motorists came to blows. It will also continue tomorrow in Iraq, Afghanistan or a London street where a crazed Islamist teenager in the name of Allah blows up a dozen innocent people who have never harmed him or the worship of his religion.

Conflict is raging invisibly but with all too obvious consequences between the greed of global corporations and Earth's fragile systems. This conflict touches us all and may wholly and fatally change our lives within a few years. That's why we all, individually and collectively, must learn to handle and resolve conflicts. Every time we succeed we have neutralized one atom of the monumental violence and hostility blighting the world. Is that too little? No, it isn't. Everything counts. The global situation is deteriorating – climate change, overpopulation, loss of fertile soil, pollution, energy shortages – and so it's vitally important to create a zone of peace and stillness around us. Anger is contagious; so are radiant goodwill and peacefulness, only they work more slowly and less visibly.

What causes conflicts? What kind of energies fire them?

First of all, the will to power and the urge to control may cause trouble, or else some unrelated frustration may seek compensation through involvement in conflict. Either way, how is one to deal with it?

While anger – both yours and mine – is contagious, in itself it is not bad and will not vanish as a result of our inner development. Anger is energy and resembles electricity, in that it can support life or be a killer; the question is the purpose for which we use it. According to the American psychologist Abraham Maslow, one of the founders of Transpersonal Psychology, once a certain level of consciousness has been reached, anger undergoes a change; it turns into energy, self-defence, just indignation, determination, resistance to all that is negative and support for all that is good and useful.

Our first and hardest task is to defuse our anger; not deny or repress but defuse it, because we know and feel that it doesn't belong here. We do not pick up the symbolic gauntlet that invites us to fight a duel. This is far from easy. Even the body reacts vigorously if it feels attacked. If I am travelling on the crowded London Underground and someone unintentionally pushes me aside with a heavy backpack, my elbow flies out sideways equally involuntarily to protect me – and shove my assailant. This reflex hasn't changed since we last carried a flint hammer and wore animal pelts to keep warm.

However, let us try to avoid this if it's not a matter of being accidentally pushed aside. What are we to do?

First of all, we should not get carried away by strong feelings when the conflict is initiated by the other party. (Hence the classic reply of the schoolboy when the teacher asks him why he is fighting with his schoolmate: 'It all started when he hit me back.') An effort is needed to switch off the hostile feelings: they prevent a satisfactory outcome. These days people quickly lose their cool. We exist in a quagmire of frustration, tension and unexpressed anger, so that the mildest provocation can make the volcano erupt. Thus it's all the more important to remain calm and not catch the infectious anger.

Next, we need to learn what this is all about. If I am being criticized, is the criticism justified? This, too, can only be decided coolly, not in a state of red-faced indignation. If it is justified, I have to accept it, but I should also suggest that we discuss matters calmly. If it is unjustified, I should say so. What is essential is to continue communicating and keep to the subject.

Try to separate the person from the problem. This helps to avoid a clash based on mutual personal attacks and insults. I have no problem with *you*; it's just that our views are rather different. And I refuse to see your attitude as a personal attack on me, even though you may have intended it to be that. I simply refuse to play your game.

If the other person sounds sharply hostile, try to separate his or her wish or suggestion from the tone being employed. Long experience has taught me that anger and rage weaken and fade if they are not fed by the opponent's anger. This is akin to the Japanese martial arts technique used when a much stronger opponent rushes towards you ready to attack but in the last second you calmly shift sideways, so that he is floored by his own momentum, while you quietly walk away.

Now comes the decisive move: to listen to each other and to try to bridge the gap between the two poles of the conflict. As a rule, with some exceptions, neither party is entirely wrong or entirely right.

This is where the possibility of a compromise first emerges, but it's still very fragile and must be handled with care.

It is this mutual listening to each other that is missing from most conflict situations, bringing on the danger of each partner spouting his or her monologue and not hearing the other. The great Austrian philosopher and author Martin Buber has formulated a theory about human relationships that refers to this danger. He defined two kinds of relating.

The first is 'I and You'. This stresses the mutual holistic existence of two individuals. The authentic selves of the two meet unconditionally, acknowledging their meeting.

The second is 'I and It'. Here there is no meeting of two individuals. The 'I' defines and qualifies the other as a thing that can be used for his or her own purposes. There is no dialogue, only a monologue.

Conflicts, altercations normally belong to Buber's second example: two monologues resound next to each other, and neither is heard until we begin to listen. And, once the listening has started, we will be able to relate in a new way to our fellow beings, to our nearest and dearest as well as to the unpleasant stranger.

To live at a higher level of consciousness is our essential aim. Several esoteric traditions suggest that soon our Earth will undergo a significant change, and concurrently we humans also need to change and raise our awareness in order to cope with this cosmic event.

All of us need to fulfil this task individually. But at least now we know that we are not alone.

5
Midlife – Crisis or Renewal?

As a rule, the period between the ages of thirty-five and forty-five is seen as a tricky or even critical one: it means that youth – and with it the first half of life – is definitely over. However, the Chinese ideogram for crisis consists of two parts, meaning 'danger and opportunity', which is a very accurate description of what we are dealing with. How we react to it is a different matter. The collective expectations are largely gloomy, assuming ageing and ever faster decline, yet these are not mandatory. It's up to us how we deal with this new chapter. Some see the problem as a matter of changing appearance and have a go at artificial rejuvenation. Thanks to the tricks of the cosmetics industry, women can easily postpone the visible signs of ageing.

Men sometimes cling to objects that rightly belong to their vanished youth. For example, an acquaintance of mine celebrated his fiftieth birthday by acquiring a stunning and very expensive sports car. Unfortunately getting on and off the low seat turned out to be painful for his aching back and knees. After suffering silently for a few weeks he swapped the car for a less sexy but more comfortable one.

The wise solution is to accept what there *is*, in other words practise what I call the Janus Moment. Janus was the ancient Roman god who appears on antique coins as a double profile, looking in opposite directions; in his sanctuary in Rome he was worshipped as the god of beginnings, entrances and exits. I regard him as the god of midlife, because he looks both backwards and forward, which is exactly what we need to do, linking the past and the future in the present moment.

Here is what Jung had to say on the subject. 'It is a great mistake to think that life becomes meaningless when youth and growth come to an end. Life's afternoon is as significant as its morning, only its meaning and aim are different. However, if someone carries over the aims and laws of youth into life's afternoon, he or she will pay for it by suffering psychological harm, just like the adolescent who attempts to extend the selfishness of childhood into adult life will suffer social failure.'

He divided life's symbolic map into two parts, each

with its own aim. First comes establishing a career and a family, followed by discovering the non-material spiritual values and conquering the inner world.

This is how he summed up his insight. 'That what we found in our youth in the outside world must be discovered within ourselves in life's afternoon.'

In other words, we need to link the inner and outer worlds, keep both feet on the ground but be aware of the non-material spiritual dimension. We need to feel liberated, laugh freely, enjoy life's gifts and handle its difficulties wisely.

Following the backwards glance of Janus, let us recall what we were like between the ages of eighteen and twenty-five and ask three questions:

- At the time did we have any idea of what we would like to achieve in the future?
- Did this wish come true, wholly or in part?
- If it didn't, can anything be salvaged from that original dream?

Another purpose of pondering the past is to learn from our mistakes, non-judgementally, as wise, objective observers. Let's remember a past event that we would rather ignore and again ask three questions:

- What should have been done differently?

- Would it have been possible to act differently?
- Is there any unfinished business that needs considering?

We cannot change the past, but we need to evaluate it, not judge it with today's awareness. We are the ones who cling to all the negative stuff, yet midlife is the time to accept the past and let go of old hurts and disappointments, whether we have caused or suffered them. If we can make amends, let's do it. If we can't, let's do it in imagination.

Then there is the important area of values. As a rule we inherit them from our parents and wider family; not just material values but also our view of the world and of life in general. If these suit us, there is no problem, but as a rule they don't: generational differences, a changed lifestyle and altered possibilities intervene. At midlife we need to examine our set of values: which ones we can accept and which ones we have grown out of or never felt comfortable with and can now discard.

'The unexamined life is not worthy of a human being,' wrote Plato 2,500 years ago. Let us live consciously, even if the outcome is negative and we are confronted with reality: youth is finally over, what comes next is ageing and eventually death. That's heavy stuff –

it implies decline, loss of good looks and a general shrinkage in all areas of life. But it's up to us whether we accept the collective expectation of what will happen at a certain age.

Because age can be assessed in different ways, as I know from personal experience. A friend of mine decided at the age of thirty-five that she was now elderly and began to behave and dress accordingly. I watched with alarm how fast she was 'ageing', while her contemporaries were in full bloom. At the age of fifty she became seriously ill and died a year later. By contrast, I recall an old family friend who celebrated her eightieth birthday by declaring, 'I don't have much of a future, but I do enjoy the present.' She died at the age of a hundred and one.

I am not claiming that the difference between those two cases was solely due to expectation, but it's a scientifically proven fact that our prevailing mood, expectations and view of the world do influence the functioning of the immune system: a positive attitude strengthens, while a negative one weakens the immune system, which is our first-line defence and should be taken great care of.

Energy follows thought. It's up to us whether we dance or shuffle towards life's afternoon. All we need to give up are our negative expectations. Life's second half should be a time of harvesting and sowing seeds. Let us harvest and enjoy the fruits of our development so far. As for sowing seeds, having given birth to our children or our creative achievements, we now give birth to ourselves in the richest and most complete form we can.

What do we need for that? First and foremost, we have to improve our relationship to our body. As a rule, we take better care of our car than of our physical vehicle. The metabolism slows down – we would need more exercise and less but better food, but normally we do the opposite and as a result slow down and put on weight. It's not cruel fate but our ignorance that causes the trouble.

The body is a miraculous precision instrument. Every cell has its own wisdom and activity. Just consider how spontaneously a wound heals: all we do is clean and bandage it, but the healing itself is done by the body. Also note how food is converted into energy, strength, or – in the worst scenario – indigestion. If we observe, understand and support the body's autonomous functioning, we shall enjoy a big health dividend.

Possibly our looks are not as good as they were at the age of twenty, but they may be more attractive, irradiated by our more mature inner self and increased understanding. The famous Italian actress Anna Magnani said that past the age of forty everybody has the face he or she deserves. She didn't allow her photographs to be retouched, claiming that her lines and wrinkles were part of her biography.

On the intellectual level, the brain, the thinking function, needs constant challenges and nourishment. It's not true that our mental ability inevitably deteriorates after midlife. The brain has a huge extra capacity and is able to replace the dead cells, provided that we keep it active. Albert Einstein, the towering intellect of the twentieth century, declared, 'I have no extraordinary talents, but I am passionately curious.' Yes, we must always have something that strongly interests, excites or angers us, something new to learn or to discuss. I once saw the following notice on the door of a big office: 'When did you last have an original thought?' That's a question I often ask myself.

We need to live at the intersection of time and timelessness and ask what the truly important things are in life. Trivial nonsense must be discarded, for instance, the negative inner voices that want to silence the positive and creative ones. We all know these inner voices. The Nattering Cynic criticizes, ridicules and dismisses everything. The Strict Judge scares us and undervalues our best efforts. The Victim complains that they've cheated and harmed me again; what else can I expect? The Guilty Soul regrets having done the wrong thing again. The Angry Ego shouts, 'I'll show them. I'll have my revenge!'

We have many inner voices – most of them not our own. The Judge and the Victim are the worst. We carry them from childhood when they seemed perfectly natural, but now we need to find out whose voice often commands us, that of the strict or of the martyred parent? Both may cause harm.

It's time to get rid of the voices of the past. It's simply done: you listen to the voice and then politely reply, 'Yes, I've heard you, but now I decide what to think, not you.' And also, 'I've heard this already, there's nothing to add.' Every time the inner voice starts up, this is what we reply, until one day the implanted voice falls silent and our own voice begins to speak.

This is nothing less than taking charge of our inner world and expanding it. We accept ourselves, with humility and humour. 'This is what I am like now. I accept it but it's not for keeps, I'm working on it.' This has advantages. We are not trying to show an artificially perfected personality to the outside world. We don't depend on the approval of others. We hope they'll accept us, but this doesn't influence our behaviour. If during the first half of life we always adapted to the expectations of others, now is the time to change direction.

And we must learn to laugh more, spontaneously and in a totally liberated way.

6

Second Flowering

The arrival of midlife deserves to be celebrated. It's a symbolic mountain peak offering a wide horizon from where we can examine the past and plan the future, even though that is still hidden by a discreet mist, only letting us indulge in assumptions. However, the celebration and planning need to be followed by simple questions: for instance, where exactly do we go from here, what may we realistically expect from the next few decades, are we able to affect our future life or must we allow circumstances to shape it?

It's largely up to us what the passing of time brings along: aimlessness, a creaking, aching body and a sad soul or wisely maintained good health, inner freedom, serene peace and the exploration of new possibilities; in other words, a second flowering of body and soul. All it needs is an open mind, willpower, a little self-discipline and a well-nourished sense of humour.

To start with, let us discard the collective expectation that beyond a certain age the only way to go is downhill. Politicians and sociologists often talk about an ageing population, including a growing number of pensioners, and they raise the question whether in the near future there will be enough working-age people to support them. This sounds like a veiled reproach to those beyond a certain age: how come you are still alive? It reminds me of the Eskimo practice of putting elderly members of the tribe on ice floes and letting them float to the next world. Fortunately nothing like that is practised in our part of the world – and not only because of the scarcity of ice floes.

At the same time, youth is seen as the highest value: it equals beauty, vast energy, perfect health, unlimited possibilities, an infinite future – at least according to the advertising industry and the sages of Hollywood. It has almost become a duty to remain young, come what may, which has brought about the incredible development of the beauty industry and of new medical procedures: surgical slimming, Botox, hormone therapy (which may cause cancer) and facelifts. And one can add to that the huge range of age-defying products, special foods, supplements, potions and more. Unfortunately the relevant advertisements feature only beautiful young women who don't need the stuff they are trying to sell.

As for the fashion industry, it produces some remarkable outfits that are both infantile and sexy that mainly suit the under-fifteens. Men's clothes tend to be modelled by sulking, barely post-adolescent youths; women's by a similar age group of young beauties who, unlike the males, are all smiles. It seems to most of us that in the modelling world success belongs solely to the under-twenties.

These are the symptoms. What lies behind them? Well, the consumer society is used to having a wide choice of everything – but in this area there is no choice; the passing of time and of life itself cannot be stopped. And the consumer doesn't like this one little bit, because he or she is afraid of old age and of death. But this isn't consciously accepted, either, so there is no way to deal with the fear.

At least in Britain older people are less often excluded from the job market, for the reason that many young people are unable to spell or count without the aid of a computer. They download the information they need from the internet and may not know how to undertake research any other way. Sometimes one feels that they would rather gaze at the screen of their smartphones than communicate with fellow humans. Business leaders are beginning to admit that older people may be the better workers. They were brought up to work hard, and they can generally write and add up without relying on computer spellchecks and calculators.

On the one hand, these days we live longer, and two-thirds of our lives pass after the end of youth. On the other, youth is generally seen as the greatest good. This dichotomy must be resolved and updated: the prevailing paradigm is obsolete. It comes from a time when human life expectancy was short: the upper limit stood around forty years. Shakespeare's Juliet was due to be married at the age of thirteen before she fell in love with Romeo. There were epidemics and conflicts; many women died in childbirth; men waged wars; life was uncertain and fragile; ageing started early. Some of this pattern cast its shadow over even the twentieth century: my own mother, as an attractive and healthy thirty-year-old, felt that she was elderly, her life as a woman was over, there was nothing to expect. She lived to the age of eighty-nine.

Sigmund Freud believed that women's destiny was shaped by biology: only their fertile years were of significance, and during those years they had no choice; their job was to produce babies. That is no longer true either.

The facts have changed, although the collective outlook

still lags behind. To change it we are encouraged to 'not just add years to life but also add life to the years'. That's our job here and now – to add vitality, colour, goals and joy to the extra years, to change the current paradigm, the view of the world that serves as the base of an all-embracing theory.

We must change the paradigm which claims that after a certain age the only way is down, towards physical and mental decline, weakness, uselessness, sickness, more and more needs and less and less vital force. This collective expectation is powerful, almost hypnotic, so that eventually we accept what deep down we know to be untrue.

The older generation need to rebel and act against this belief. If society doesn't value our age group, we need to value ourselves, casting assumptions aside. As a rule we don't do that; women are particularly at fault here. From the beginning of time, women have been expected to live for others, to serve them and to take care of everyone except themselves. Many nineteenth-century authors, especially Dickens, wrote with great approval of inhumanly perfect, unselfish and self-sacrificing heroines.

Such generous service is needed within the family – but for a limited time only. Later the offspring, by now young adults, either exploit their mothers, for instance, by turning them into full-time grandmothers and unpaid carers, or they move away for good, leaving behind emptiness and the pain of absence. For men it's loss of work, for women it's loss of family that hurts most. Many women need to be needed, which shows a caring attitude but also signals that without serving others they have no sense of self and self-worth. That equals a lack of identity and autonomy, plus a need for others to validate their right to exist; hence they are unaware of their own possibilities and strengths.

This needs to be recognized and acknowledged. What looks like emptiness is, in fact, a space full of new possibilities. We create the major part of our reality, so it's up to us what we choose. According to the writer Anaïs Nin, 'We don't see the world as it is but as we are.' We all have some unlived life, some missed or stolen possibilities; now is the time to utilize them and take full advantage of our remaining time. It's precious time and our own.

As a rule, neither men nor women prepare themselves for the great change that follows midlife, the trauma of retirement or of the 'empty-nest' syndrome. Yet without proper preparation these can cause a great decline, sudden ageing and aimlessness. Again, men find this harder to bear; women always find something to do – even if it's not the right thing.

Our aim is a second flowering. The first occurred naturally, as a gift of youth. The second one we have to create. The flowers will be different, perhaps dahlias instead of daffodils, but they should be perfect. This doesn't mean denying reality, mortality, the ravages of time or the losses caused by ageing. All that is part of the package. But we can cultivate our garden, look after the flowers and enjoy life.

The task must be approached at the body–mind level, as the two are inseparable. Let us start with the body, because that is where ageing usually first becomes noticeable, and if we don't deal with it wisely sooner or later it'll become all-important, pushing all else aside. Here, too, we have a choice: are we going to drag along an aching, creaking body, full of prescribed drugs that often don't work, or do we treat the body well, so that it can become our best ally, provided that we listen to it and give it what it needs?

In the arena of health we will encounter a powerful assumption that as we age we encounter a range of diseases that can neither be avoided nor cured. That is not true, but as our doctors largely accept this melancholy theory most people believe it. From analgesics to digestive aids, in Western society we consume vast quantities of drugs and nutritional supplements, and since some of them clash with each other the results are often unsatisfactory. Of course we need drugs but only within sensible and necessary limits. (I recall undergoing a medical checkup some years ago and the doctor asking me what drugs I was taking. 'None,' said I, upon which he sighed and replied, 'So that's why you are so well.')

What makes us ill or at least not healthy? A combination of harmful habits, an overload of stress and time-poverty. In the first half of life the organism is able to protect itself; later its resistance weakens, the immune system runs down and in due course a range of troubles arise: these may include rheumatism, arthritis, insomnia, poor digestion, heart or kidney irregularities, the threat of diabetes and of malignant disease. 'It comes with age,' the exhausted doctor assures the unhappy patient and prescribes a drug that deals only with the symptoms but leaves the causes untouched.

Today's health problems are often described as diseases of civilization, and indeed we seem to have forgotten that we belong to Nature. Our development over millions of years progressed through slow natural processes, but the

Industrial Revolution shattered these, and in the past seventy-odd years our environment and our food have undergone drastic changes. The impoverished soil of industrialized agriculture produces nutritionally poor but richly sprayed crops which are then 'refined' to our detriment by the food industry. As a consequence, more and more of us are overfed but undernourished, half healthy and half sick, half poisoned by agro-chemicals, with reduced immunity and energy.

For this reason a growing number of people choose a different path by eating organic food and consulting qualified naturopaths and other alternative practitioners when the need arises. The global food industry is too rich and powerful to regard this as a serious threat, which is fine – at least our freedom of choice remains safe.

It's a fact that simple but thorough dietary changes can eliminate many chronic symptoms of sub-optimal health. All we need to do is take responsibility for our health, maintaining or restoring it, according to its current condition, and avoiding the mass hypnosis practised by the consumer society.

The origin of 'diet' is the Greek word *dieta*, which means a total lifestyle or way of life, including one's eating habits. To get it right, it's not enough to avoid a few foods of dubious value: a total change is needed, in the spirit of getting back to nature. Today's over-refined and highly chemicalized foods are both toxic and deficient in nutrients. The toxicity is caused by the food industry, which uses some 3,000 so-called 'food cosmetics', the purpose of which is to replace by artificial means the natural flavours, colours and aromas lost during the manufacturing process. We need to eliminate these and substitute wholesome ones, which generally means buying and preparing nutritionally rich organic produce. Granted, this takes longer than popping a ready meal in the microwave oven, but the extra effort is a long-term investment in good health.

There are certain misguided attitudes that can annul our good intentions:

- The belief that cooking good food just for oneself is a waste of time;
- Comfort eating; sadly the consoling foods and drinks – cake, chocolate, alcohol – merely pile on weight but do not heal a sore heart;
- 'It's all the same now', the enemy of healthy vanity. Let us follow the example of Freud's mother who remained slim, elegant and pretty all her long life and, aged ninety-two, complained that a photograph of her made her look old.

We must pay attention to our body, regard it as a valuable partner, not a subordinate machine, and notice when it's tired or has aches and pains. Popping a pill is usually not the answer. We also need to accept that we may not look as attractive as in our youthful prime but in our latter years have a beauty that radiates from within – provided there *is* something to radiate. As time passes, the body needs more and more support. But don't let us spoil or over-indulge it; above all, don't let us identify with it in health or in sickness. The vehicle is not the driver, and we shouldn't mistake the ceiling for the sky.

The life of the great Swiss psychologist Jung is a good example of an intellectual and spiritual second flowering. In his sixties he barely survived a severe heart attack but wrote some of his most important works after his recovery. He tackled life's fundamental problems in his ancient tower home overlooking the lake at Zurich, but at the same time he liked to eat well, drink good wine and enjoy the beauty of nature.

At the age of eighty-four, two years before his death, he gave a moving interview for BBC Television, in a film that has since become a classic, revealing Jung as a wise old man.

This is the advice he gave to elderly people. 'It's good

if an older person approaches every new day as if he were to live for ever on this earth. That way he lives properly. But if he is frightened, if he doesn't look ahead, only back, then he'll become rigid and die before his time. But if he looks forward confidently to the great adventure awaiting him, then he is truly alive.'

As our life expectancy these days is pretty high, youth accounts only for a third or even a quarter of our lifespan. Yet all kinds of education and training are solely focused on that third, meaning that we need to live through the remaining two-thirds in a state of unpreparedness. Little wonder that most people are worried about their later years, while a daring minority quietly but powerfully rebel against social or even family-based assumptions and create for themselves a second flowering.

In the process of ageing, gains and losses are closely linked. No need to describe the losses; they are only too familiar. Instead, let us recognize and enjoy the gains, the many new freedoms we couldn't have imagined in our younger years. We see clearly and are able to release our past crises and traumas. We no longer want to please everyone. We are able to love without dependency. We are able to love ourselves and develop the huge gifts of tolerance and a sense of humour: with their help the once threatening risks suddenly become very small.

A wonderful illustration of that process came from the American actor Bob Hope when he said, 'At the age of twenty my big worry was what other people thought of me. At forty I decided that whatever they thought I'd do things my way. At sixty I discovered that nobody ever thought anything about me.'

In that spirit let us fully enjoy the many gifts of our second flowering.

7

The Art of Uncluttering

These are critical times, a period of transition, when any idea of the future is bound to be unreliable. The twin problems of climate change and overpopulation raise the question of whether a part of humankind will be destroyed by natural catastrophes or by famine, as if our planet wanted to strike a balance between the necessary and the possible with one almighty shrug. At least for the past hundred years we have been consuming Earth's resources faster than they could be naturally renewed, which is destroying the very foundation of human existence and means that sooner or later the much vaunted 'consumer society' will consume itself. Fortunately more and more people realize what's going on, and many remedial actions are gaining strength worldwide. The problem concerns both individuals and the collective. As an individual I cannot expect others to solve our problems. In the words of Jung, 'If there is something wrong with society, then there is something wrong with the individual, and if something is wrong with the individual, then there is something wrong with *me.*' The task awaits us all.

Even a journey of ten thousand miles begins with one step, claimed a Chinese sage of long ago. He might have added that you, as the traveller, know what needs to be done. Journeys are dangerous undertakings, hence we must ensure that however many apparent certitudes fall by the wayside we preserve our inner certitude and move forward towards an enhanced consciousness. That will give us the necessary strength, inner peace, fortitude and tranquillity, whatever happens around us. In other words, we'll be able to see what is going on from a higher, non-ego-ruled point of view, while keeping both feet firmly on the ground.

If we want to make good progress, we need to ask 'What is holding us back?'

In a miniature Zen story the dead-tired pilgrim collapses at the feet of the Master and asks, 'Master, why am I so exhausted?' The Master replies, 'Why are you carrying that big sack of stones on your back?'

What does the sack of stones symbolize in our lives? Everyone has a different answer to that question, but one thing is certain: most of the stones come from the past and belong there, yet we continue to carry them. And that is dangerous: it endangers life's greatest treasure, the present. Why do we allow this to happen?

Sometimes an external episode provides the answer to an internal question. A friend of mine once helped her mother to discard a load of things that had become useless clutter, but after she had left her mother recovered the stuff which she saw as treasure, not clutter. Some of our belongings that were once useful and valuable but aren't either any more become a kind of treasure that we keep, apparently for ever. Yet they take up a lot of space. The clothes went out of fashion ages ago; we certainly won't reread certain books; the old, tired towels no longer absorb water; yet there they remain. We badly need to reclaim a few shelves or drawers – but do nothing to clear them. Why not?

The items may come in handy, we think, yet we suspect that they won't. Those who grew up in times of hardship or shortages hang on to things that their children would have chucked out long ago. But there is another reason for keeping them. Almost all old belongings are witnesses to our past – not like a journal, not like photographs or video films, but by way of association. I believe that women are more likely to hoard such mementoes; they keep the high-heeled sandals they can't wear any more and the hideous hat and the tasteless mock-folksy bag they bought in Greece a decade or more back, because each of these objects conjures up memories and confirms the reality of the past.

It is true that men also cling on to certain objects, such as badly worn pullovers or battered briefcases, but for them that tends to be more a matter of habit, rather than a sentimental memory. All of this boils down to an unconscious attempt to build a protective wall around our fast-moving daily lives and keep the past alive by preserving its debris.

A friend of mine told me the other day that she has three large holdalls full of ancient letters, postcards, theatre and concert programmes, paid bills and photographs. 'Why are you keeping all that?' I asked, knowing how small and overcrowded her flat is. 'I want to go through it all when I'm an old lady,' she replied, adding that her ex-husband's letters are highly unpleasant and will no doubt upset her again, but that if she threw them away there would be a big hole in her past, which she didn't want.

This is a good example of how we attempt to use objects to ring-fence the past, to prove that I've been there, that's what I was like, this is mine, no one can take it from me. However, if – like my friend – we also retain objects that hurt, infuriate or trouble us with negative feelings, we should stop and ponder what is going on.

Because here we move from external clutter to the internal kind, which is the real goal of our quest. All of us, without exception, since our earliest age have been absorbing everything that's been going on around us, adding to it our reactions and feelings, letting the material accumulate, but it is invisible and so we do not notice the process. Of course plenty of good, valuable and beautiful stuff is also part of the whole, enriching our life and brightening our days.

However, we are concerned with the psychological clutter and rubbish that we all collect, starting in child-hood when we are small and weak and at the mercy of all-powerful giants, namely the grown-ups. And some-times the giants, often inadvertently, hurt us. The psy-chologist Alice Miller has written that what the adult regards as a joke may be a severe upset for the small child, who feels offended, hurt and made ridiculous. What can the child do? If it's small, it can burst into tears. Later this is no longer possible, so it swallows the real or imagined offence but doesn't forget it.

What makes things worse is that in the human psyche there is an embedded and inherited expectation – an archetype in the Jungian sense – of the ideal mother and ideal father. The ideal mother represents unconditional love; she is tender, warm, nourishing, protecting. She is safety itself. The ideal father is strong and respectable; he lays down the rules and laws, he teaches and guides, initiates his child into worldly affairs, encourages it and sets up expectations. At the same time, he is under-standing and fair.

These are archetypes. Such ideal parents don't exist, but the small child doesn't know this and feels disappointed when its expectations are not fulfilled: when Mummy is too busy to play with the child or Daddy shouts in annoyance because his offspring has yet again knocked over the milk jug. All such negative experiences or even joking reproaches go deep. Then there's more to come, more severe parental chiding, angry, thoughtless com-ments such as 'You useless kid, you've made a mess again. You'll never be any good', and so on, essentially calling the child worthless and inadequate and adding that of course its brother or sister knows how to do things correctly.

What happens next? The child either rebels and proves

its ability to succeed in its next task or it gives up before even trying. Either way the parental chiding and scorn are stored in the database of the psyche, and the humiliated child living within us never gets rid of them.

This is how the accumulation of negative psychological clutter began in childhood. We now have to excavate an inner situation which we wouldn't otherwise contemplate or of which we may not be aware. Sometimes that in itself produces a solution as we gradually remove the symbolic sack of stones from our back. It's a do-it-yourself way to free up our inner world.

Doing this matters, because the unrecognized negative clutter directly influences our behaviour and expectations, as well as how we react to given situations and relate to others. It belongs to the past but has the power to cast its shadow over every aspect of our daily life.

There is a harmful habit that most of us indulge in until something forces us to recognize and abandon it: namely, to guard the vivid memory of everything that failed us in the past, everything that hurt, angered, distressed us many years ago, our major and minor defeats, our unexpressed love or unspoken truth, and every time a ghost from the past appears we re-experience our pain or rage of long ago. We spend much less time recalling the beautiful, serene and uplifting events of the past; little wonder that after a while we become sour and disgruntled.

This needs changing but not by trying to repress all our negative memories – a forlorn effort anyway – but by focusing on the positive ones and noticing the pleasant moments of the here and now, however small they seem. There is a simple way to anchor them: all it needs is a notebook, plus keen attention to everything that is happening to and around us. Every day for two weeks we record positive events on the left-hand page, negative ones opposite, and every evening add up the result on both sides. Often we will find more positive than negative experiences, especially towards the end of the two weeks. It's not that the world has changed, nor have our fellow beings become nicer: we have simply learnt to notice and appreciate the countless small gifts of every day.

It's a small gift if a toddler smiles at you for no good reason or if a healthy weed pushes up from a crack in the pavement – proclaiming that there is life beneath the asphalt and that it's strong enough to break through. Or you go to the bus stop, resigned to waiting for fifteen minutes, but the bus arrives at once. Yes, small things but good ones, and if we give ourselves permission to enjoy them the inner–outer atmosphere of the moment improves noticeably.

But why do we cling to our painful or depressing memories? Note that we are doing the clinging; they can't cling to us. This is the first fact to acknowledge. Next, it's up to us whether we let them go or continue to preserve them. Often the storing of old hurts is motivated by self-pity. There's nothing shameful about that; just that it's a total waste of time. The inner monologue goes like this: if nobody is sorry for me I'll do it myself. I am an unjustly treated victim; the person I most trusted has hurt me most, and so on. At this stage the martyr complex may emerge, offering the bonus of self-justification to the tune of 'I'm decent, I'm honest, yet everyone hurts and exploits me'.

Somewhere in the background the Zen Master asks, 'Why do you put up with it?'

Zen Masters are not impressed by self-styled martyrs. Of course there are genuine ones, and they do suffer. But in many cases the victims themselves attract the exploiting and unloving people, often family members, who treat them badly. Don't let us underestimate the power of expectations. Every thought, every feeling has its own energy. If I expect to be misused and hurt, that's what will happen to me.

The power of expectations is one of life's unrecognized yet strongest energies, and we constantly and unconsciously radiate our expectations. Others automatically and just as unconsciously receive the message, and thus we react to each other. It is as if all of us were dual-function radio stations, sending and receiving programmes. This doesn't mean that maintaining positive expectations attracts nothing but good things, but the number of bad experiences will certainly decrease.

Another negative habit is to preserve past hurts and use them as a weapon against their perpetrator. This normally happens within the family, when the wife says to her husband – or the reproachful mother tells her grown-up child – something along the lines of 'And three years ago, that time when you said to me . . .' Three or more years have passed since then, the other party has long forgotten that episode, but the offended individual remembers it vividly and attaches it to the current problem by way of reinforcement. Never mind that it has nothing to do with the current situation; the main thing is to embarrass the other person. Yet we shouldn't judge this technique too harshly; it's often used by those who lack self-confidence and feel the need for this kind of support. As a rule it doesn't work. It may even exacerbate the conflict.

Old painful memories may also be kept alive to serve as self-defence. Two or three love affairs had gone badly, causing much heartache, so from now on the heart will be excluded from intimate relationships.

This is how the not fully conscious decision-making process goes, but at any rate it doesn't work. Incidentally, this is a female speciality, and the woman who uses it is like the Ice Queen from the fairy-tales; she has locked up her heart in a foolproof safe and thrown away the key. All along those ancient disappointments serve as a background. What never occurs to the Ice Queen is that it was she who chose two or three partners unable to maintain a happy relationship.

That's enough to start with. Let's turn inwards, relax, become still. If we, like most of us, are carrying inner clutter, why are we doing it? What is it for? And why shouldn't we start getting rid of it here and now?

A final thought: whatever belongs to the past cannot do us any harm, unless we cling to it and let it overshadow the present.

The French artist Serge Poliakoff might have had uncluttering in mind when he said, 'If you seek perfection, don't ask what you need to add to what you are doing but what you need to remove from it.' He was referring to paintings, but the same principle works well to cleanse our inner world, too.

8

And Then? End or Beginning?

At some stage of life we are all confronted with the subject of death, which these days is generally avoided, as if by ignoring and denying it we could escape its reality. According to the concise definition of the Austrian philosopher Ivan Illich, 'Death is the consumer's final resistance.' Indeed, sometimes it seems that only through this drastic step can we escape from the incessant hubbub and superficial values of the consumer society.

Death has been humankind's abiding mystery since the beginning of time. Each ancient civilization had a different approach to the subject, including the conflict of mortality and immortality. Christianity offers a clear solution, claiming that after death, according to what it deserves, the immortal soul finds itself in a rewarding or punishing situation. I have to confess that even as a small girl I thought the reward of eternal light and rest sounded eminently boring, more akin to a punishment, but I kept this view from our terrifying priest-teacher who disliked me because I tended to ask questions instead of meekly accepting his every word. Well, yes, I wanted to find out more, but the priest did not appreciate this. Many years later I was delighted to read that Einstein, one of the towering geniuses of our time, always emphasized his curiosity and flatly denied having exceptional talents. (It should be noted that I am *not* trying to set up a parallel between Einstein and myself.)

For many centuries, if not millennia, death was almost always represented – especially in Europe – in the same terrifying form, as a skeleton wearing a black cloak and carrying a scythe, cutting us down as it pleased. World literature offers countless wonderful references to the subject, including Shakespeare's 'undiscover'd country from whose bourn no traveller returns'. Except that this isn't true any more.

The change came in the early 1970s with the great improvement in medical techniques of resuscitation, so that many more patients could be brought back to life after a severe heart attack or other life-threatening emergency that had briefly left them in a state of clinical death. Their numbers kept growing, and many began to talk about their experiences. Eventually an American physician, Dr Raymond Moody, collected over a hundred reports which turned out to be amazingly similar.

In brief, the doctor declares the patient to be dead. However, the patient – whose brain appears not to function any more – hears a strange noise and at the same time moves fast along a long dark tunnel. He notices that he is no longer in his physical body. At the end of the tunnel he reaches a light place where he sees several of his dead friends and relatives who welcome him with joy. Then a Being of Light, radiating love, appears and asks him whether he wishes to return to his life on Earth. He would prefer to stay in the afterlife but knows that his family and his work need him, and so he travels back speedily through the tunnel.

Moody's book, relating these stories, appeared in 1975 under the title *Life After Life* and quickly became a global bestseller. It introduced the concept of the Near-Death-Experience or NDE and launched an avalanche of research by doctors, psychologists and sociologists. More books kept appearing on the subject, and this began to transform the conventional collective ideas about death, which no longer seemed to be a final catastrophe and total extinction. These changing ideas were aptly expressed by

Dr Elisabeth Kübler-Ross, one of the pioneers of the new attitude, in the following words. 'Death is the final stage of growth in this life. There is no total death. Only the body dies. The self or spirit, or whatever you may wish to label it, is eternal. You may interpret this in any way that makes you comfortable.'

Taking as my starting point the adage 'Life is a journey that doesn't begin with birth and doesn't end with the death of the body', I believe that those who strive to develop their consciousness are making progress in this timeless area. If we need to re-evaluate death, we must do the same with life and with our relationships to each other.

The great American writer Thornton Wilder ended his classic novel *The Bridge of San Luis Rey* with this sentence: 'There is a land of the living and a land of the dead and the bridge is love, the only survival, the only meaning.'

Yes, the bridge is love. And so the only answer to my question can be 'There is only a beginning – and infinity.'

Books Cited in the Text

Buber, Martin, *I and Thou*, T. and T. Clark, Edinburgh, 1937

Illich, Ivan, *Limits to Medicine: Medical Nemesis*, Marion Boyars, London, 1975

Jung, Carl Gustav, *Psychological Reflections: An Anthology of the Writings of C.G. Jung*, Harper Torchbooks, New York, 2001

Kübler-Ross, Elisabeth, *Death: The Final Stage of Growth*, Prentice-Hall, Englewood Cliffs, New Jersey, 1975

Maslow, Abraham, *Toward a Psychology of Being*, D. Van Nostrand Company, Princeton, New Jersey, 1962

Miller, Alice, *The Drama of Being a Child*, Virago Press, London, 1987

Moody, Raymond, *Reflections on Life After Life*, Stackpole Books, Harrisburg, Pennsylvania, 1971

Nin, Anaïs, *Delta of Venus: Erotica*, Harcourt Brace Jovanovich, New York, 1977

St Exupéry, Antoine de, *The Little Prince*, Reynal and Hitchcock, New York, 1943

Wilder, Thornton, *The Bridge of San Luis Rey*, Albert and Charles Boni, New York, 1927

Winnicott, Donald, *Playing and Reality*, Tavistock Publications, London, 1971

Peter Owen Publishers

info@peterowen.com

@PeterOwenPubs
Facebook: Peter Owen Publishers

Independent publishers since 1951

www.peterowen.com